Work
— YOUR —
Purpose

**A BOOK OF REFLECTION FOR WOMEN WHO DESIRE
TO CONNECT TO THEIR PURPOSE**

By Shannon Wilkerson and Tomika Haynes

Work Your Purpose
A Book of Reflection for Women
Who Desire to Connect to Their Purpose

Shannon Wilkerson
Tomika Haynes

© 2019 Shannon Wilkerson Tomika Haynes
Work Your Purpose: *A Book of Reflection for Women Who Desire to Connect to Their Purpose*

ISBN: 978-1-64606-329-1

Printed in the United States of America

CONTENTS

Introduction

Let me ask you this...

Have you ever said to yourself "There has to be more to life than this!"? I have. That was my inner purpose questioning my mediocre life and telling me that God has a plan and a purpose for me. I was not, at that time walking in it and was no longer content just existing. I wanted to walk in my purpose and the plans that God has for me. I wanted what He wanted for me!

Don't get me wrong, all things work together for those who believe. So, even when I wasn't walking in my purpose, God was still orchestrating my movements and guiding me back to His plan. I was just taking the scenic route. However, in those moments of questioning, I didn't feel good about my current state of being and desired more.

I had done a lot of good. I had advocated for a lot of families as a Family Support Specialist, helped a lot of children reach their educational goals as a Teacher, served in my church and volunteered my time and money to charitable organizations, but had not fully discovered the reason for my existence. Like a lot of people, I was in the seeking phase. In this phase you can achieve some level of success, but still may not be in alignment with your purpose.

It is possible to find yourself unhappy even within a situation that a lot of people would envy. Think of the rich people who have committed suicide or died from a drug overdose looking for an escape from their inner demons. Meanwhile, others think that being rich would solve all of their problems. True happiness is only found within a quality relationship with your Creator and knowing His plan for your life. This is often the missing piece that creates the missing peace.

Now, when I say "quality relationship' understand that God is always holding up His end of the deal. It is you and I who sometimes fall short. We need to take the time to nurture this relationship that

He has made available to us. So, if the relationship is falling short, it's because you have yet to realize that it is a two way relationship. Yes, God will continue to love and bless you, but there is so much more to God than that. Don't you want everything that God has to offer? Isn't it your desire to know what He has planned for your life?

I want nothing more than for you to realize that you were created with great purpose and to seek God to gain the knowledge of your purpose. He will give you the blueprint to work it! Stop living a life of frustration, fear, hurt, turmoil etc. That's what the world and its ways has for you, but that's not what God has for you. This workbook will lead you through a process of self -discovery and reflection that will guide you closer to God and erase all confusion about who you are and why you were born.

Please do record your thoughts and write out your plans. The Bible says *"Write the vision, and make it plain"* Habakkuk 2:2, (Amplified Version) Make your plans real to you! Then turn your plans into goals and goals into accomplishments. Let go of whatever is holding you back from being amazing!

As a bonus, I have partnered on this project with my good friend Tomika Haynes because I firmly believe that we are not meant to do life alone and I want to spread the message of women coming together in support of one another, understanding that my light won't dim yours and vice versa. Most importantly I believe in what she has to say and I know that it will bless you!

Pick your crown up and be free to walk in your purpose,

Shannon

THERE'S NO COMPARISON TO YOU!

It is far too common for women to measure their own value based on another woman's accomplishments, her family unit, the way that she looks, her income etc. If we could only see ourselves how God sees us, how awesome would that be? Everyone's purpose is different. So, why are you constantly comparing yourself to other women and constantly fighting for a position. God has already placed you where He wants you to be. You don't have to fight for it! It's yours!

Don't look at other people's glitter and (sometimes fake) gold and feel like you're behind in your journey. Instead look at how far God has brought you. Remember when you couldn't pay your bills or when you were still in that bad relationship that was clearly not for you? Look back on that and laugh. Laugh at the devil and how he tried to hold you back from living in your purpose.

Maybe you are currently still in that place. At any time you can change your situation. You have the tools to do it. *"Death and life are in the power of the tongue." Proverbs 18:21* (Amplified Version) Speak life into your situation and shine the light on the dark places! Use your words to affirm and encourage yourself and your decision to make better choices. Don't look back! Your Purpose lies ahead!

Most importantly, remember that there is only one you. Many of us are blessed with similar talents and gifts that align with our purpose, but only you can work that purpose the way that you do! Instead of comparing yourself to someone else, focus on being the best possible you. That's when you'll be able to shine your brightest.

EVERYONE'S PURPOSE IS DIFFERENT. SO, WHY ARE YOU COMPARING YOURSELF TO OTHER WOMEN AND CONSTANTLY FIGHTING FOR A POSITION? GOD HAS ALREADY PLACED YOU WHERE HE WANTS YOU TO BE!

Reflect & Change

What has God said to you about your purpose and His plan for your life? If you are unclear, go to God in prayer and write what He says to you.

_____

_____

_____

_____

_____

_____

_____

_____

_____

_____

_____

_____

_____

_____

_____

_____

_____

_____

WHAT DO YOU WANT TO SEE

At some point we have all sat down and planned our lives based on what we thought we wanted or needed. Some of our plans were actually placed in our hearts by God Himself and others we thought up on our own. Either way, we had plans. The thing about plans is that in order for them to become real, we have to do the work.

We can't just hope and wish for things. Hoping and wishing without action will not result in you getting what you want. We have to learn to attract to our lives what we want to see and experience. So many people wake up every day dissatisfied with what they see around them because it's not how they visualized their life, but do nothing to change it.

How many years are you going to live in a neighborhood that you don't like? How long are you going to stay on that job that you hate instead of seeking a new opportunity? When are you going to start taking action and making changes? You are not powerless to change your current situation. You just have to make a decision to do something different.

Fear can no longer paralyze you if you want to live a purposeful life. You have to conquer the fear that has held you back. Fear has a way of looking like other things. A lot of Christians remain in the same position year after year by allowing fear to disguise itself as "waiting on God". In many cases we are not waiting on God! He's waiting on us!

WE HAVE TO LEARN TO ATTRACT TO OUR LIVES WHAT WE WANT TO SEE AND EXPERIENCE.

Reflect & Change

You can't be inconsistent with your efforts and actions and still expect change. What steps will you take immediately in order to see what you want in your life?

_____

_____

_____

_____

_____

_____

_____

_____

_____

_____

_____

_____

_____

_____

_____

_____

NUGGETS TO LIVE BY

What we are able to produce and attract to our lives is directly influenced by what we are meditating on. Consider these things...

1. How many hours this week did you spend watching tv? What were you watching?

   _____

2. How many hours this week did you spend listening to music? What type of music were you listening to?

   _____

3. How many times have you opened your Bible this week other than at church on Sunday?

   _____

4. Did you take time to pray today?

   _____

What will you do differently now that you've reflected on your habits and daily routines?

_____

_____

_____

BELIEVE AND YOU WILL RECEIVE

Whenever I set a goal for myself, I create a "purpose board" to help me visualize it. I use that purpose board and my journal to create a plan which includes the action steps to achieving the goal. Then I pray and ask God for it. From that point on, the goal is set. Now I start acting like I already have that thing that I have planned for and prayed about. Why? Because God is going to make it happen! I am so confident in that fact that I talk about it like it's already mine and even make plans as if it's already done.

Let me give you this example. I set a goal this year to earn $30k above what I earned last year. As I planned for this year and mapped out financial strategies and investments, I included the extra $30k that I know is already on its way. Here we are halfway through the year and I am on track to meet this goal.

What are you believing God for? Are you bold enough to plan for it? Will you rejoice like you've already received it? Are you expecting it? See, there is a major difference between wishing and expecting. When you are expecting, you are confident. You speak differently. You aren't speaking doubt and unbelief. You speak like someone who is ready to receive.

Someone once said to me that I am lying to myself to pretend like I already had something that I did not have in my possession. I quickly corrected him stating that I am not "pretending". Clearly this was a non-believer. As Christians we know what the Bible says in 1 John (Amplified Version) that *"This is the confidence which we have before Him: that if we ask anything according to His will, He hears us."*

16

WHENEVER I SET A GOAL FOR MYSELF, I CREATE A VISION BOARD TO HELP ME VISUALIZE IT. THEN I PRAY AND ASK GOD FOR IT.

Reflect & Change

What are you believing God for? What promises has God made to you that you need to pick back up and believe for?

_____

_____

_____

_____

_____

_____

_____

_____

_____

_____

_____

_____

_____

_____

_____

_____

_____

_____

_____

_____

DIG DEEPER

So many people get caught up in their own outward appearance and become so consumed with how others see them. They diligently work on improving what the world sees, while neglecting the inward part of themselves, the part that is broken. We have to make sure that we are not improving ourselves only on the surface, but that we are making deeper inward improvements.

It is great to look nice and to be seen as beautiful, intelligent, fashionable, successful etc, but what about what is happening on the inside of you? Is that not important too? It is actually most important. You can be the most successful broken person there ever was and never truly discover your purpose.

Being the best possible you is not about how you look or how you are viewed in the eyes of others. It involves how you feel about yourself, who you are as a person, the impact that you have made in other people's lives and being at peace with yourself. It's about waking up every day, looking in the mirror and being happy with the woman that you see.

If there are parts of you that do not reflect the image of God, work on that. It's never too late to change. Take the time to examine your own heart and ask God to remove anything that is not like Him. Watch how God will continue to mold you into who He has called you to be! You will be unrecognizable!

WE HAVE TO MAKE
SURE THAT WE ARE NOT
IMPROVING OURSELVES
ONLY ON THE SURFACE,
BUT THAT WE ARE
MAKING DEEPER INWARD
IMPROVEMENTS.

Reflect & Change

How much time do you spend thinking about who you are on the inside and the purpose that God has placed on the inside of you? Do you like what you've discovered about yourself? Are you in position to live in your purpose or are there things that you would like to change?

_____

_____

_____

_____

_____

_____

_____

_____

_____

_____

_____

_____

_____

_____

_____

_____

_____

_____

_____

NUGGETS TO LIVE BY

You can be the most beautiful woman in the world on the outside, but if you are inwardly a mess; you will still turn people off.

Give an example of this

_____

LOSE CONTROL

Let's settle this right now! You are the daughter of a King. That makes you royalty. As a royal, you have access to everything that you need to live a successful and happy life. The thing is, sometimes you go about life as if you don't know that. You can't believe when it applies to one area of your life and then doubt when it comes to other areas. Its either black or white. Either you believe or you don't.

My issue was that I could easily believe God for things that I felt were beyond my control such as my health, but I wanted to control the things that I felt I could and would not ask God about those things. I would just do my own thing. For instance, I could control what jobs I accepted, where I wanted to live, how I managed my money, who to date etc. So, those areas of my life were all about me and my choices. God was not consulted at all, but when those choices led me down the wrong path, I would cry out to Him for help.

Does this sound familiar? Are you still trying to maintain control over your life? The power struggle is real, right? Sis, just let it go! Let it go and let God. You will find peace in that place of knowing that God has it under control and will only set in motion what is right for you. Trust God with your whole heart. Allow Him to lead you and direct your path. Life gets so much easier that way. You can take this ride in total peace knowing that God has taken the wheel.

AS A ROYAL, YOU HAVE ACCESS TO EVERYTHING THAT YOU NEED TO LIVE A SUCCESSFUL AND HAPPY LIFE.

Reflect & Change

What things do you need to release from your own hands and give to God to take care of for you? Think about things that you have been stressing over or watching too closely. Start there.

_____

_____

_____

_____

_____

_____

_____

_____

_____

_____

_____

_____

_____

_____

_____

_____

_____

_____

WHAT ARE YOU SPEAKING?

Why did God give us the ability to speak? I believe it's because He wanted us to speak things into existence, speak life into dead things, to affirm ourselves and to use our voices to praise. Somehow this got twisted and we started to use our voices to kill our own dreams, to speak negatively about ourselves, to gossip about others and to hurt one another.

Are you saying what you want to see in yourself, your situation and in other people or what you currently see with the natural eye? The world believes only what they can see in the natural, but as a believer we believe what God has promised. Make a choice to speak those promises! Say "I am healed, I am wealthy, I am happy, I am the righteousness of God". Remind yourself daily what God has said about you.

Before you speak over yourself, your children, your spouse, your job etc, ask yourself if what you are about to say is going to feed a problem or create a solution. We all want solutions in our lives. So, why feed the problem? Don't let your own words trip you up. Make up your mind to speak life!

Even from a natural perspective, this concept is the same. If you tell yourself something enough, you start to believe it and your mind and body respond to it. For example, if you are always talking about what you don't have and what you can't do, you will likely never have or do those things. Your mind and body will become stressed and you may find yourself depressed or even physically sick over time. Where did this begin? With your own thoughts and words.

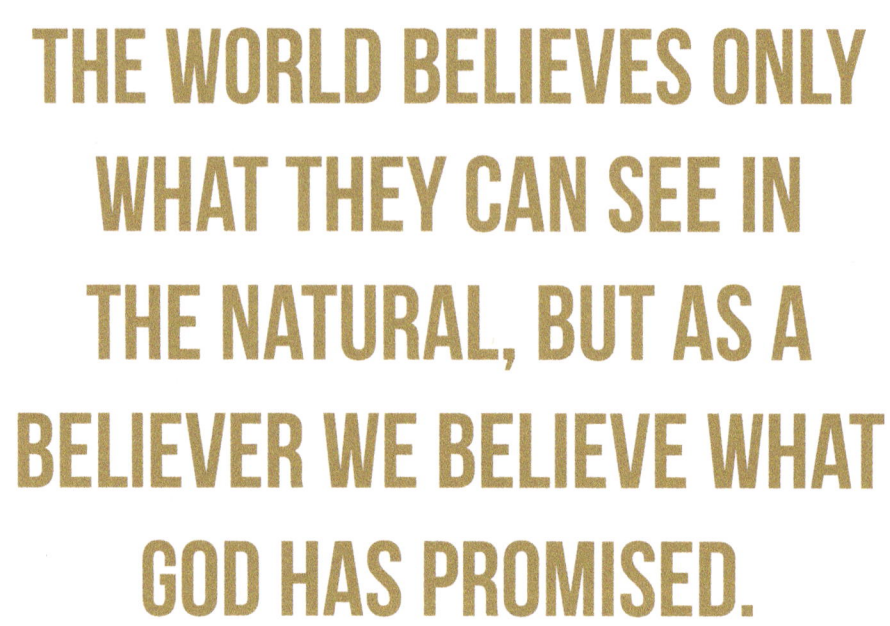

THE WORLD BELIEVES ONLY
WHAT THEY CAN SEE IN
THE NATURAL, BUT AS A
BELIEVER WE BELIEVE WHAT
GOD HAS PROMISED.

Reflect & Change

Write 5 positive affirmations that you will speak over yourself every day. Post them on your refrigerator, on your bathroom mirror or any other place where you will see it often. Read them out loud frequently.

NUGGETS TO LIVE BY

Affirmations are only helpful if you believe them. Find things that you genuinely like about yourself and start there. Seek the truth of what God has to say about you and look for those qualities in yourself. It's in there!

Document your thoughts here as you go through this process.

_____

_____

_____

_____

_____

_____

_____

_____

_____

_____

_____

_____

_____

_____

_____

_____

_____

_____

SPEAK OVER YOUR SISTER

One of the biggest joys in my life is to be able to put a smile on the face of a woman who doesn't feel supported and loved. It is awesome to be able to share God's love with someone and to make them hold their head up a little higher with some positive words. When you feel good about yourself, it is much easier to love other people and to spread the positive vibes that are on the inside of you. When you take away the need to compete, there's space for genuine love for your sister.

So many women are hurting and could use some words of encouragement. We should be seeking opportunities to speak life into other women. If not for you, they may otherwise never hear kind words about themselves. Take your mind off of yourself and your circumstances to focus on someone else. There you will find a blessing. God *said "This is My commandment, that you love and unselfishly seek the best for one another, just as I have loved you." John 15:12* (Amplified Version)

Your kind words could mean the difference between life and death for someone. I am sure that you have heard stories of people on the brink of suicide until God sent someone to share His love with them and it completely turned the situation around. Wouldn't you like to be a part of something like that? What an amazing thing to know that you saved someone's life just by extending kindness.

34

WHEN YOU TAKE AWAY THE
NEED TO COMPETE, THERE'S
SPACE FOR GENUINE LOVE
FOR YOUR SISTER.

Reflect & Change

In what ways can you be supportive to another woman in or even outside of your circle? What impact do you think this support will have on her life?

_____

_____

_____

_____

_____

_____

_____

_____

_____

_____

_____

_____

_____

_____

_____

_____

_____

_____

_____

UNBROKEN

As women we have the ability to be strong and fearless. Nobody can break us unless we allow them to. We are not defeated by a loss or by what may look like a failure. We pick ourselves up, regroup and get right back to it. This is what makes us amazing! It's our superpower! Sometimes life has a way of making us forget this, but we can't stay down! Getting up is a must!

Have you ever felt like you've been dealt an impossible hand? I know the feeling. I have had to overcome several trials in life. Some of them were harder than others and some definitely took longer to overcome. However, I made it to the other side of it and learned several lessons in the process! Are you still fighting battles? Does it still feel impossible to win? What are you fighting with?

You cant fight life battles with wishful thinking. You have to fight with the Word of God! Find the right scriptures to take to combat and meditate on those scriptures day and night until you see what you want to see. During this time of studying the Word and prayer, don't stress over the battle. God is fighting for you!

Whenever you are faced with a difficult circumstance, go to God first. Many times we want to ask other people for their opinion or advice. Its nice to have people to talk to, but don't forget God in the process. He has all of the answers and unlike people, His answers are always right.

WE ARE NOT DEFEATED BY A LOSS OR BY WHAT MAY LOOK LIKE A FAILURE. WE PICK OURSELVES UP, REGROUP AND GET RIGHT BACK TO IT.

Reflect & Change

Go to God in prayer regarding the things that concern you and write down the practical strategies that you can implement right away.

_____

_____

_____

_____

_____

_____

_____

_____

_____

_____

_____

_____

_____

_____

_____

_____

_____

_____

NUGGETS TO LIVE BY

Finding your inner strength to regroup and continue on your path is essential because life will throw many curve balls at us. How have you found your inner strength in past situations?

_____

_____

_____

_____

_____

_____

_____

_____

_____

_____

_____

_____

_____

_____

_____

_____

_____

_____

_____

_____

BREAKING TIES

There are times in our lives when we have to evaluate our personal relationships and connections. This can include business associates, friends and even family. Not every relationship is meant to be long term and not everyone is meant to be in our inner circle. Some of these relationships may be blocking us from discovering our purpose or fully living in it. Some things we can't obtain while maintaining connections to things that we need to let go of.

Have you ever known someone to do extremely well in business, career, personal life etc. after leaving a relationship that wasn't good for them? Usually, God has already spoken to us and told us to walk away from the person, but we did not immediately listen to His voice. God patiently waits for our obedience so that He can release everything to us. Many times we ask for things that we are not yet ready to receive and wonder why it has not been released to us. Some people even blame God when in actuality He is doing what is best for us at that time.

It does matter who connect yourself with. In my own personal life I have had to break ties with people who were negative talkers. I realized that their negativity was seeping into my heart and mind and keeping me from my purpose. They were making deposits of unbelief, doubt, and fear in every conversation. Walking away brought such freedom and my faith grew instantly. I then replaced them with people who were constantly speaking life into me. They were saying what God was saying. Things started happening for me at a much faster pace because I was so full of faith.

43

GOD WON'T GIVE YOU CERTAIN THINGS WHILE YOU ARE CONSUMED WITH DISTRACTIONS THAT WILL CAUSE YOU TO NOT HANDLE PROPERLY WHAT HE GIVES YOU.

Reflect & Change

Are there people or things that you need to disconnect from? Why is it important that you do so? What impact do you think disconnecting will have on your life?

_____

_____

_____

_____

_____

_____

_____

_____

_____

_____

_____

_____

_____

_____

_____

_____

A ROSE IS STILL A ROSE

Just like flowers, daughters of God have many purposes. We are beautiful and add beauty to the world, but what we often forget is, flowers are even more useful after they have been crushed. The crushing produces oil and perfumes that lasts longer than the beauty of the flower.

Although we may not realize it and it doesn't feel like it while we're going through hardships in life, after these crushing experiences is when our purpose is produced. The healing powers of a flower are the most potent after they are crushed.

What the enemy means for bad, God uses for good. *"As for you, you meant evil against me, but God meant it for good"* Genesis 50:20 (Amplified Version) When we learn how to heal ourselves and let the experiences teach us we can turn it into purpose.

The things you have gone through in life may make you feel weak, but there is strength in doing as instructed in the Word. We must renew our minds and change our perspective so that we can turn the crushing experiences into transformation. Just like a flower that has been crushed, we feel and look ruined but what really happens is that more power is released.

After many emotionally crushing experiences throughout my life, I realized that once the tears had cleared I had to take my focus off of the pain and focus on what I had gained. Look at how you've survived and, what you've learned. Turn your mess into your message.

Wisdom Holistics

47

THERE'S ALWAYS A PURPOSE
BEHIND THE PAIN. YOU
BECOME EVEN MORE
POWERFUL WHEN YOU'VE
GONE THROUGH SOME
THINGS.

Reflect & Change

Think about the crushing experiences that you have lived through. What "superpowers" did they produce in you?

_____

_____

_____

_____

_____

_____

_____

_____

_____

_____

_____

_____

_____

_____

_____

_____

_____

_____

_____

_____

NUGGETS TO LIVE BY

Your strength will often surprise you and appear just when you need it! Think about the strong women in your life. What makes them strong in your opinion?

_____

_____

_____

_____

_____

_____

_____

_____

_____

_____

_____

_____

_____

_____

_____

_____

_____

_____

LET IT MAKE YOU NOT BREAK YOU

The heartbreaks that I've experienced throughout my life, made my perception of people very jaded. I had a hard time trusting other people because I was always expecting more of what I'd received in the past. Because I allowed these experiences to shift my thinking, even when good things would come my way, I would sabotage it as a defense mechanism. The bible says *"For as a man thinks so is he." Proverbs 23:7* (Amplified Version

I allowed fear to drive my thoughts and action. Because of what was going on in my heart, my perception was off. So, I would end up manifesting exactly what I feared. Until I learned how to heal internally and change my perception, I repeated this cycle over and over again.

Trauma no matter how big or small will have an effect on our lives until we heal from it. The smallest things can bring the biggest pain and in most cases without us even realizing the affects. Pain can mold and shape who we are and how we perceive others and the world around us.

Our individual pain and experiences matter. I encourage you to seek help from a spiritual leader or professional counselor if necessary to get to a healthier emotional place. The things we go through in life can break us, but they can also make us into who God created us to be. It's up to you!

Wisdom Holistics

THE FIRST STEP TO TURNING PAIN INTO PURPOSE IS TO RECOGNIZE THAT THERE'S A WOUND.

Reflect & Change

What unresolved wounds have you not addressed and how have they shaped or molded your perception of yourself and the world around you?

_____

_____

_____

_____

_____

_____

_____

_____

_____

_____

_____

_____

_____

_____

_____

_____

_____

_____

HE STILL LOVES US

Life has taught me that we are not what happens to us and our mistakes do not define who we are and what we can have. Our mistakes can sometimes make us feel unworthy of all the good that God has for us. Our negative experiences can make us feel like God has forgotten about us, but that is simply never true. We are His children and He is a good daddy!

Our circumstances can manipulate us into thinking that the cards we've been dealt are the only cards that we can play. This creates cycles of negative experiences. It can even trick us into believing that the things that happen to us, we somehow deserved. That is a trick of the enemy to keep us in bondage and keep us from declaring what God has said about us.

God has a plan and a purpose for us and He doesn't change His mind when we make wrong decisions. He doesn't think any less of us because of our mistakes. Don't you still love your children when they make mistakes? Well, God loves even better than we do! His love is unwavering. God will take the things that happened to you and use it to make things happen for you! *"If you then, evil as you are, know how to give good gifts to your children, how much more will your Father who is in Heaven give what is good and advantageous to those who ask."* Matthew 7:11 (Amplified Version).

GOD WILL TAKE THE THINGS THAT HAPPENED TO YOU AND USE IT TO MAKE THINGS HAPPEN FOR YOU!

Reflect & Change

What actions can you take today to stop the negative cycles in your life? How can you get back on track with God's vision for your life?

_____

_____

_____

_____

_____

_____

_____

_____

_____

_____

_____

_____

_____

_____

_____

_____

_____

_____

_____

NUGGETS TO LIVE BY

A cycle is only a cycle if we keep it going. We can at any time break cycles. What are some of the cycles that you have/ have not yet broken?

_____

_____

_____

_____

_____

_____

_____

_____

_____

_____

_____

_____

_____

_____

_____

_____

_____

_____

WHO YOU REALLY ARE

Sometimes our past experiences cause us to forget who God created us to be. This common identity crisis is what causes many people to live outside of the will of God and to be caught up in a lifestyle that is not what He intended for us. When you get to the point of realizing who God has called you to be and start to grow into that person, you'll go through a pruning phase.

This phase can be painful because in the beginning, we don't yet understand that the things that we appear to be losing in the process are not really losses. Those things are not in alignment with who we are and not worthy to be compared to what God has for us. These things, or even some people in our lives, are not connected to our purpose.

I used to be one of those people who would do anything in my power to keep something old working. One time I took apart an old DVD player that stopped working, just to avoid getting a new one. After I saw how much DVD players had changed and all the new options, I said to myself, "why did you waste your time trying to make that old one work." Sometimes things no longer work because God has something better. You have to stop piecing the old things back together and let go.

61

GOD USED THAT TO SHOW ME
THAT SOMETIMES THINGS
NO LONGER WORK BECAUSE
HE HAS SOMETHING BETTER.
LOSING THINGS DOES NOT
ALWAYS MEAN YOU'RE
LOSING.

Reflect & Change

What are some things that you've been holding onto that's been slowing you down from discovering and living in your purpose?

_____

_____

_____

_____

_____

_____

_____

_____

_____

_____

_____

_____

_____

_____

_____

_____

_____

_____

NO MORE SHAME

There is freedom in knowing how God sees you and what He has to say about you. Armed with this knowledge, you can no longer be held captive to shame or doubt. Nothing you've done and nothing that's been done to you can steal your value. You are still precious to God.

Shame is one of the chains that keeps you tied to your past and in bondage. It will cause you to hide things that need to be uncovered so that you can start your healing process. Let go of shame and activate the power of forgiveness. Forgive yourself and move forward. Once you do that, there will be a shift that occurs on the inside of you and you will gain back your power.

Once you release shame, you not only empower yourself. You create a light that shines on others who are hiding in the dark because of their shame. You become a light carrier. People who struggle with what you once struggled with, will flock to you and God will use you to set them free.

The Bible says in *Revelation 12:11* *"And they overcame and conquered him because of the blood of the Lamb and because of the word of their testimony"* (Amplified Version) Your past gives you a testimony to use to break the chains holding others captive. Your story is not just about you.

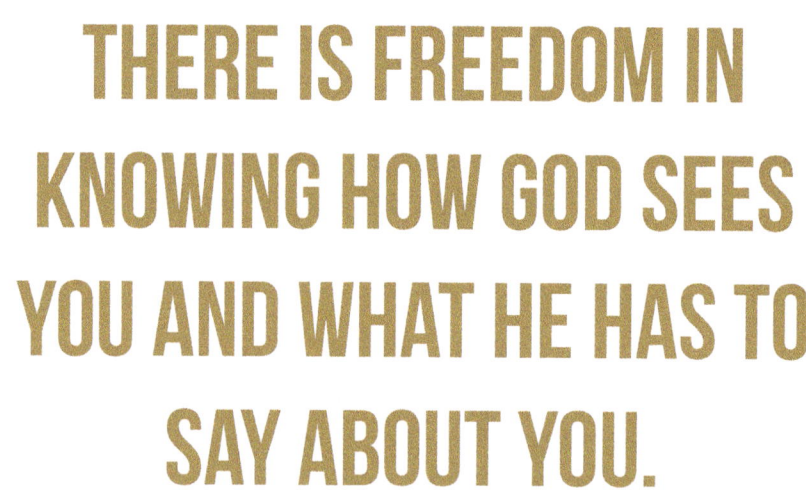

THERE IS FREEDOM IN KNOWING HOW GOD SEES YOU AND WHAT HE HAS TO SAY ABOUT YOU.

Reflect & Change

Are you harboring feelings of shame? What do you need to release yourself from? Now, replace those things with what God said about you.

_____

_____

_____

_____

_____

_____

_____

_____

_____

_____

_____

_____

_____

_____

_____

_____

_____

_____

_____

_____

NUGGETS TO LIVE BY

Once you become free from shame, others can break free? What part of your story do you think will have the biggest impact on the lives of others?

_____

_____

_____

_____

_____

_____

_____

_____

_____

_____

_____

_____

_____

_____

_____

_____

_____

_____

BUILD YOUR PURPOSE WITH THE PROCESS

There is a common phrase "pain leads to purpose", but what people fail to see is there is an entire process between pain and purpose. It would be more accurate to say when you learn what the pain is teaching you, then will you be led to your purpose. That's how our negative experiences can be used for our good and God's Glory.

It's easy to focus on what happened and what you could have done differently. It's okay to reflect but to solely focus on your pain can keep you stuck in the emotions surrounding what happened. It's imperative that you learn how to shift into a place of healing so that you fully operate in your purpose.

Focusing on the lessons learned and the process in between pain and purpose will get you closer to your goals. What you learn from the things that have happened in your life, you will later teach. This not only goes for the painful things in life, but your successes too.

THE LESSONS YOU'VE LEARNED HOLD MORE WEIGHT THAN THE MISTAKES.

Reflect & Change

What lessons are to be learned from your past experiences?

_____

_____

_____

_____

_____

_____

_____

_____

_____

_____

_____

_____

_____

_____

_____

_____

_____

_____

OLD WAYS CAN'T OPEN NEW DOORS

You can't make your purpose fit into your old life. Change is required. You can't fully experience a life of purpose with the same mindset, behavior and methods that you used before. This has been proven to be true on so many levels in my life. The way we operate, think and behave must change when we're on the mission to live out the purpose and destiny God has for our lives.

Your path to purpose requires new decisions and actions that serve the person you're destined to be and not the broken person that you once were. If you don't implement these new strategies, you will find yourself repeating some of the same cycles you've worked so hard to come out of. *"No one puts new wine into old wineskins; otherwise the wine will burst the skins, and the wine is lost" Mark 2:22* (Amplified Version)

When you start to make changes that serve the new you, people will start talking. It's okay. We've all had to go through that phase. Many people will not receive the new, better version of you and will even remind you of who you used to be in an effort to make you feel like you haven't or can't change. Stay focused!

YOUR PATH TO PURPOSE REQUIRES NEW DECISIONS AND ACTIONS THAT SERVE THE PERSON YOU'RE DESTINED TO BE AND NOT THE BROKEN PERSON YOU WERE IN THE PAST.

Reflect & Change

Can you identify the past decisions and actions that have led you down the wrong path? What can you do differently?

_____
_____
_____
_____
_____
_____
_____
_____
_____
_____
_____
_____
_____
_____
_____
_____
_____
_____
_____

NUGGETS TO LIVE BY

Changing your habits will take time. The key is to be consistent. What will keep you consistently working towards creating new habits? What's your "why"?

_____

_____

_____

_____

_____

_____

_____

_____

_____

_____

_____

_____

_____

_____

_____

_____

_____

_____

TRUST GOD AND WORK THE PROCESS

Getting through the pain and healing is a process of prayer, research and soul work. Not only is it a process it's a cycle of growing, learning and healing. Everything that we go through prepares us for the next phase. We can choose to go through things, or we can choose to GROW through things. These are two totally different cycles and we must choose which one we want to be in.

The difference between the two is one keeps you moving forward, and one keeps you starting all over again and again. You may have heard "You won't pass the test until you've learned the lesson." This is true, but this saying is missing one of the steps. After we have learned what the process has taught us, we must apply the lessons learned to our current and present situations.

We can move through hard circumstances with much more ease when we apply what we've learned in the past. God never promised us that life would be easy, but He did promise that we would be able to endure the process. Take what you've learned and use it to keep moving forward.

DON'T JUST GO THROUGH THINGS GROW THROUGH THINGS.

Reflect & Change

Do you see a connection between things that you have gone through in life and how it prepared you for a future life experience?

_____

_____

_____

_____

_____

_____

_____

_____

_____

_____

_____

_____

_____

_____

_____

_____

_____

_____

GOD'S WILL IS THE WAY

We often have our own step by step plan for our lives not realizing that God had our destiny planned before we were even born. When I think about all the things I've fought against, held onto or just flat out refused to do because I wanted to follow my own plan, all I can do is shake my head. (Hindsight is always so much clearer).

When we follow our own plans and not God's plan, it causes more growing pains than we have to experience. God will allow us to pursue our own ambitions, but still use it for His original purpose. We do our own thing, fall down, and scrape our knees a couple times unnecessarily. Like any good Father, He brushes us off and sets our feet back on the path and we start again. Thank God for mercy!

Surrender your plans over to God in exchange for His plan for your life. Watch how much easier things will become. When you fully trust God, you can live a worry free life waking up every day wondering what adventure He will take you on next!

SURRENDER YOUR PLANS
OVER TO GOD IN EXCHANGE
FOR HIS PLAN FOR YOUR
LIFE.

Reflect & Change

Write a note to God telling Him that you surrender to His plan for your life and that you fully commit to trusting His plan during your journey.

_____

_____

_____

_____

_____

_____

_____

_____

_____

_____

_____

_____

_____

_____

_____

_____

_____

_____

NUGGETS TO LIVE BY

Life experiences have taught some of us that vulnerability leads to pain. What would you say to someone (or yourself) who struggles to be vulnerable before God and to rely on Him totally?

_____

_____

_____

_____

_____

_____

_____

_____

_____

_____

_____

_____

_____

_____

_____

_____

We hope that you have enjoyed the journey that we have walked you through in this workbook and are closer to discovering and walking in your purpose!

If you are interested in coaching services, please reach out.

We would love to hear from you!

Shannon Wilkerson, Business & Writing Coach
Shanniwilke.com

Tomika Haynes, Transformational Coach
Wisdomholistics.com

CPSIA information can be obtained
at www.ICGtesting.com
Printed in the USA
BVHW021804020719
552333BV00002BA/7/P

9 781646 063291